OXYGEN

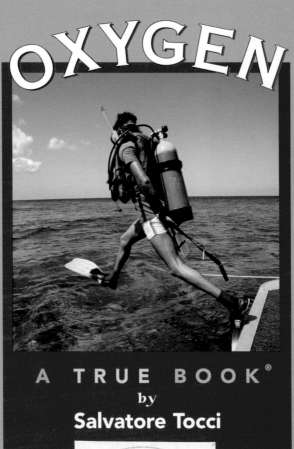

A TRUE BOOK®

by
Salvatore Tocci

Children's Press®
A Division of Scholastic Inc.

New York Toronto London Auckland Sydney
Mexico City New Delhi Hong Kong
Danbury, Connecticut

Three things are needed to make fire: heat, oxygen, and fuel. Without oxygen, there can be no fire.

Reading Consultant
Julia McKenzie Munemo, EdM
New York, New York

Content Consultant
John A. Benner
Austin, Texas

The photo on the cover shows algae producing bubbles of oxygen gas. The photo on the title page shows a diver with an oxygen tank diving off a boat.

The author and the publisher are not responsible for injuries or accidents that occur during or from any experiments. Experiments should be conducted in the presence of or with the help of an adult. Any instructions of the experiments that require the use of sharp, hot, or other unsafe items should be conducted by or with the help of an adult.

Library of Congress Cataloging-in-Publication Data

Tocci, Salvatore.
Oxygen / by Salvatore Tocci.
    p. cm. — (A true book)
    Includes bibliographical references and index.
    Contents: How far can you run?—What is oxygen?—Why is oxygen so important?—How can using oxygen cause problems?—Fun facts about oxygen.
    ISBN 0-516-22832-3 (lib. bdg.)   0-516-27851-7 (pbk.)
    1. Oxygen—Juvenile literature. [1. Oxygen.] I. Title. II. Series.
QD181.O1T63 2004
546'.721—dc22   2003016419

CHILDREN'S PRESS, and A TRUE BOOK™, and associated logos are trademarks and or registered trademarks of Scholastic Library Publishing. SCHOLASTIC and associated logos are trademarks and or registered trademarks of Scholastic Inc.

1 2 3 4 5 6 7 8 9 10 R 13 12 11 10 09 08 07 06 05 04

Contents

How Far Can You Run?

Do you like to run in races? Perhaps you race against your friends to see who is the fastest runner. Perhaps you race to see who can run the farthest. If you have run this type of race, you may have reached a point at which you had to stop running because your legs were so tired. Many distance runners, such as those who compete in marathons, have had the same feeling. Some of them felt as if they could not take another step. They call this "hitting a wall" because it feels like that is what happened to them.

One of the greatest distance runners of all times was an Australian man named Ron Clarke. In 1968, Clarke "hit a wall" during the 10,000-meter

race in the Mexico City
Olympics. Before the race
began, most people thought
that Clarke would win. Before

1968, he had broken the 10,000-meter world record three times.

During the race, Clarke was in second place and had just a lap and a half to go. He was running well and looked as if he would overtake the leader. Suddenly, Clarke stopped running and started staggering on the track. Somehow, he managed to stay on his feet and drag himself to the finish line.

Clarke obviously needed medical attention.

The team doctor rushed to help Clarke, who was unconscious and near death. For the next hour, all the doctor could do was cover Clarke with a blanket and make him breathe through a mask. Fortunately, Clarke recovered. Breathing through the mask had saved his life. The doctor had given Clarke pure oxygen to breathe.

What Is Oxygen?

Oxygen is an element. An **element** is the building block of matter. **Matter** is the stuff or material that makes up everything in the universe. This book, the chair you are sitting on, and even your body are made of matter.

Oxygen is the third most abundant element in the universe.

There are millions of different kinds of matter. However, there are approximately one hundred different elements. How can so many different kinds of matter be made up of so few elements? Think about the English language. Just twenty-six letters can be arranged to make up all the words in our language. Likewise, the approximately one hundred different elements can be combined in different ways to make up all the different kinds of matter in the universe.

The discovery of oxygen is usually credited to Joseph Priestley, who lived from 1743 to 1804. As a boy growing up in England, Priestley had no interest in science and never took any science courses in school. However, his life changed when he met a visitor from the United States named Benjamin Franklin, who was well known for his science experiments. The two became very close

Besides discovering oxygen, Priestley also invented the pencil eraser.

friends. Because of Franklin, Priestley became fascinated by science.

In 1772, Priestley made an interesting observation. Scientists knew that a burning candle placed inside a sealed jar would eventually go out. Priestley discovered that if he placed a small plant inside the jar, the candle could keep burning. Somehow, the plant had restored the air. What Priestley did not know was

Plants make oxygen and release it into the air.

that plants make oxygen through a process called **photosynthesis**.

In 1774, Priestley made another interesting observation. He used a magnifying glass to focus the sun's rays to heat a silver-colored liquid until it turned into a powder. Priestley continued to heat the powder, which evaporated into gases that he collected. One of these gases was invisible, but

Priestley knew that it was there. When he placed a glowing wooden splint near this gas, the splint burst into flames. Priestley also observed that mice became hyperactive when he placed them in this gas. What Priestley did not know was that he had made oxygen gas.

Priestley described his experiments to a French scientist named Antoine Lavoisier. Lavoisier repeated

Priestley's experiments and got the same results. Unlike Priestley, however, Lavoisier realized that the gas they had made was an element. Lavoisier named this element oxygen. Besides a name, every element has a symbol. The symbol for oxygen is O, which is the first letter in its name.

Oxygen gas has no color or odor and makes up about 21 percent of the air we breathe.

Making Oxygen

Fill a glass jar halfway with fresh hydrogen peroxide. Add 2 teaspoons of yeast to the jar. Cover the jar loosely with the lid. Look closely at the hydrogen peroxide. Tiny gas bubbles should start to form and rise to the surface of the liquid.

Ask an adult to light a small, thin piece of wood on fire. Remove the cover from the jar. Quickly blow out the flame and insert the smoldering piece of wood into the air inside the jar. The bubbles you saw in the liquid were oxygen gas that made the wood start to burn again.

Oxygen is also the most abundant element in Earth's crust, which is the solid layer that covers its surface. Most of the oxygen in Earth's crust is not found as an element.

Rather, this oxygen is found as part of compounds. A **compound** is a combination of two or more different elements. Oxygen is part of the compounds that make up the rocks and minerals in Earth's crust.

Oxygen is an element in the rocks that make up the walls of the Grand Canyon.

Why Is Oxygen So Important?

All living things need energy. **Respiration** is the process that living things use to release the energy that is stored in foods. Most people think respiration requires oxygen. However, not all living things, or **organisms**, need oxygen to perform respiration.

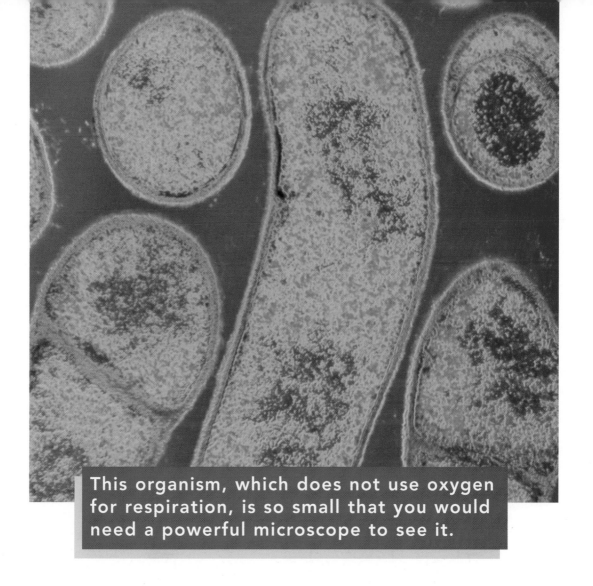

This organism, which does not use oxygen for respiration, is so small that you would need a powerful microscope to see it.

There are some living things that survive perfectly well without oxygen. These organisms

are very tiny and do not
need much energy to survive.
Respiration without oxygen
does not produce much
energy. However, the energy
that is produced is enough
to meet the needs of these
tiny organisms.

Most organisms, however,
need much more energy.
They depend on oxygen to
meet their energy needs.
Respiration with oxygen

releases almost twenty times more energy from foods than respiration without oxygen does.

The oxygen used in respiration comes from plants. You read that plants make oxygen during photosynthesis. Like most living things, plants use oxygen for respiration. Fortunately, they make much more oxygen than they use. Plants release the oxygen

Oxygen is always being recycled between animals and plants.

that they do not use into the air. Animals can then breathe in the oxygen to use in respiration. This exchange between animal respiration and plant photosynthesis is part of the oxygen cycle. The **oxygen cycle** is nature's way of recycling oxygen.

Oxygen gas is also used to make a substance called ozone. **Ozone** is a pale blue gas that has a sharp odor.

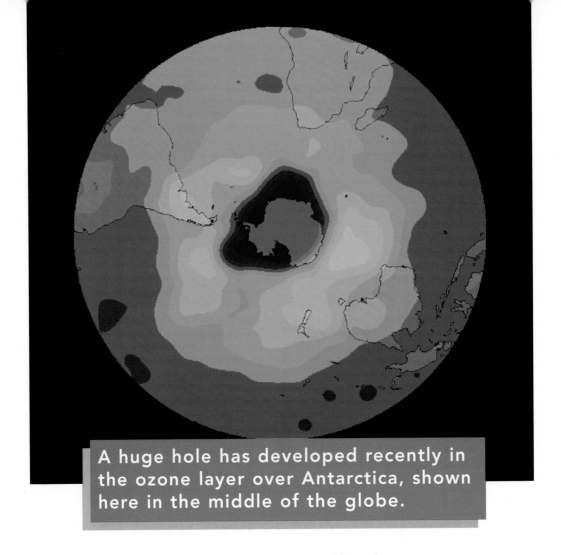

A huge hole has developed recently in the ozone layer over Antarctica, shown here in the middle of the globe.

You may have smelled ozone after a thunderstorm. Lightning changes oxygen gas into ozone. Sunlight can also change oxygen gas into ozone. A layer of ozone made by sunlight surrounds Earth. This layer is about 12–15 miles (20–25 kilometers) above sea level. It absorbs most of the harmful rays coming from the sun before they reach Earth. If these rays reached Earth, they would greatly increase the rate of skin cancer.

Football players often breathe pure oxygen to get the energy they need to keep playing.

Oxygen gas is also used to treat people. You read about Ron Clarke who "hit a wall" when he was running in the Olympics. Clarke's body had run out of oxygen. As a result, he did not have any energy to run another step. The pure oxygen gas supplied by the doctor saved his life. The oxygen was used in respiration to supply the energy Clarke needed to survive.

How Can Using Oxygen Cause Problems?

Oxygen is a very reactive element. This means that something clearly happens when oxygen is mixed with another substance. For example, some metals react with oxygen and give off a bright light.

Oxygen is reacting with this metal strip to produce a bright light.

Many substances, such as wood, gasoline, and coal, react rapidly with oxygen.

When these substances react with oxygen, a large amount of energy is released as light, heat, or sound. We call this process burning. Scientists call it combustion. **Combustion** is a process in which a substance reacts rapidly with oxygen.

Combustion has been used for ages. Early humans depended on the burning of wood to cook their food. Today, combustion is the main process through which we get

Using Oxygen

Some substances react slowly with oxygen. Soak a steel wool pad in vinegar for about five minutes. Then, pull apart the steel wool and place it in the bottom of a clear glass so that it fits snugly. Place the glass upside down in a pan of water and let it sit overnight. The next day, the steel wool should be rusted, and the water should have risen inside the glass. Rust forms because the steel wool reacts with the oxygen in the air inside the glass. As the oxygen is used up, water moves into the glass to take its place.

Gasoline reacts with oxygen to provide the energy needed to power a car.

the energy we use. For example, combustion in an engine works to move a car.

Combustion in a furnace works to heat a home. Combustion in a power plant provides electricity.

Besides providing energy, combustion also produces carbon dioxide. Carbon dioxide is a gas made of two elements, carbon and oxygen. More and more carbon dioxide is being released into the air because of combustion. Along with some other gases, carbon dioxide causes Earth's temperature to increase slightly over time. Scientists are not sure how this warming will affect life on Earth.

Car engines produce other substances during combustion that can cause problems for humans. One of these substances reacts with oxygen in the air to produce ozone. High above Earth, ozone helps protect people from the sun's harmful rays.

Ozone, which is made up of oxygen, contributes to smog.

However, here on Earth, ozone causes smog. Smog can make breathing difficult for people.

Fun Facts About Oxygen

- Liquid oxygen is used as a fuel. Each space shuttle launch burns 143,000 gallons (538,350 liters) of liquid oxygen at a rate of 17,000 gallons (64,000 L) per minute.

- The grass on a lawn that measures 50 feet by 50 feet (15 meters by 15 meters) makes enough oxygen in photosynthesis to support a family of four.

- Respiration with oxygen releases about 65 percent of the energy that is stored in foods.

- Combustion with oxygen releases about 25 percent of the energy that is stored in gasoline.

- The brain is the part of the body that uses the most oxygen. It uses about 20 percent of the oxygen that travels in the blood.

- Blood rich in oxygen is bright red. Blood without much oxygen is purplish.

- Water is a compound made of two elements, hydrogen and oxygen. Water's weight is about 90 percent from oxygen and nearly 10 percent from hydrogen.

To Find Out More

If you would like to learn more about oxygen, check out these additional resources.

 **Books**

Blashfield. Jean F. **Oxygen.** Raintree/Steck-Vaughn, 1998.

Farndon, John. **Oxygen.** Marshall Cavendish, 1998.

Malone, John. **It Doesn't Take a Rocket Scientist.** John Wiley & Sons, 2002.

Organizations and Online Sites

U.S. Environmental Protection Agency
www.epa.gov/ozone/science/missoz/index.html

Follow a reporter as he learns about why we need the ozone layer, what is causing its destruction, and some of the actions people are taking to try to correct the problem.

www.epa.gov/global warming/kids/greenhouse.html
See an animation explaining how certain gases are contributing to global warming. Learn what people can do to make a difference, such as reducing combustion.

Why Exercise Is Cool
http://kidshealth.org/kid/stay_healthy/fit/work_it_out.p2.html

Learn how aerobic exercise, or exercise using oxygen, helps the heart become stronger and even a tiny bit larger. This site also lists some aerobic exercises you can try.

Scholastic's Magic School Bus
www.scholastic.com/magicschoolbus/games/teacher/heart/

This site provides information about the heart and its role in pumping blood, which carries oxygen, throughout the body. You can do an activity to see how doing jumping jacks affects your heart rate.

Important Words

combustion commonly called burning; occurs when a substance reacts rapidly with oxygen

compound substance formed from the combination of two or more different elements

element building block of matter

matter material that makes up everything in the universe

organism any living thing

oxygen cycle nature's way of recycling oxygen

ozone substance made of oxygen that protects Earth from harmful sun rays

photosynthesis process used by plants to make food and oxygen

respiration process that releases the energy stored in foods, often by using oxygen

LAW Hold Slip
Oxygen /

Hold ID... WOO   1492

Index

Meet the Author

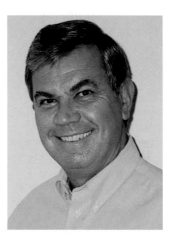

Salvatore Tocci is a science writer who lives in East Hampton, New York, with his wife Patti. He was a high school biology and chemistry teacher for almost thirty years. His books include a high school chemistry textbook and an elementary school book series that encourages students to perform experiments to learn about science. Although he has never "hit a wall," he has had difficulty breathing while skiing at high altitudes in Colorado.

Photographs © 2004: Corbis Images: 28 (Franco Vogt), 1 (Tim Wright); Getty Images/Getty News: 32; Hulton|Archive/Getty Images: 7; Nance S. Trueworthy: 16, 38; NASA: 11; Photo Researchers, NY: 14 (Biophoto Associates), 25 (A. Dowsett), 41 (D.R. Frazier), 30 (SPL), 35 (Charles D. Winters); The Image Works: 4 (Michael J. Doolittle), 2 (Steve Warmowski/Journal Courier); Visuals Unlimited: 23 (Pegasus), cover (John Sohlden).